WHO DOES HE THINK HE IS ?

WHO DOES HE THINK HE IS ?

John Marsh

Foreword by David Watson

Inter-Varsity Press

Inter-Varsity Press
38 De Montfort Street, Leicester LE1 7GP, England

Bible quotations are from the Good News Bible (Today's English Version) New Testament © American Bible Society, New York 1966, 1971, and fourth edition 1976; Old Testament © American Bible Society, New York, 1976.

First published 1982

British Library Cataloguing in Publication Data
Marsh, John
  Who does he think he is?
  1. Jesus Christ
  I. Title
  232   BT202

ISBN 0-85110-441-X

Set in 10/11 point Baskerville
Typeset in Great Britain by H.M. Repros, Glasgow
Printed and bound in Great Britain by
Collins, Glasgow

Inter-Varsity Press is the publishing division of the Universities and Colleges Christian Fellowship (formerly the Inter-Varsity Fellowship), a student movement linking Christian Unions in universities and colleges throughout the British Isles, and a member movement of the International Fellowship of Evangelical Students. For information about local and national activities in Great Britain write to UCCF, 38 De Montfort Street, Leicester LE1 7GP.

Contents

Foreword

Today, perhaps more than ever, there is enormous interest in Jesus of Nazareth. The media and the arts, for example, repeatedly return to this intriguing figure: commercially, to say the least, he is invariably a 'success'. It is safe to say that no single person in human history has been so loved or hated, so worshipped or opposed, so studied or exploited.

But who was he? The 'gentle Jesus, meek and mild' contrasts strangely with the revolutionary leader who whipped dishonest traders from the Temple precincts. He who taught 'Blessed are the meek' claimed equality with God. He who founded the greatest spiritual movement in the world was rejected by the religious leaders of his day. He whose life seemed beyond reproach was, above all, the friend of sinners. He who healed the sick and raised the dead was himself humiliated, tortured and crucified.

Who was he? His staggering claims were totally outrageous — if not true. His authoritative teaching has touched the deepest cries of the human heart in every generation. His life sums up what we would most of all like to be in our best moments. That is why those who have studied the records about Jesus have found him both inspiring yet disturbing, comforting yet shocking, compassionate yet uncompromising. In the judgments we make about him we seem to be judging ourselves.

Who was he? In this book John Marsh looks at this

controversial figure through the eyes of his contemporaries. We may find ourselves sharing their moments of astonishment or indignation. No-one could quite fit him into their scheme of things. Yet their persistent question demanded an answer: *Who does he think he is?*

David Watson

What's it all about?

A former Archbishop of Canterbury was visiting the United States. As he stepped on to American soil he was quickly surrounded by an eager group of reporters. Among the many questions which were thrown at him was this: 'Are you going to visit any night-clubs while you are in New York?'

To that, the Archbishop replied (no doubt with a twinkle in his eye): 'Are there any night-clubs in New York?'

The next morning, the eye-catching headlines in the newspapers ran: 'Archbishop's first question: "Are there any night-clubs in New York?"'

That amusing story (whether or not it's true) is a striking example of how easy it is to report another person's words accurately while at the same time giving a false impression of what was meant by them. The headlines may have been accurate enough, but because the reporter's initial question was missing, readers would get the wrong idea of what the Archbishop actually said.

Many, both the famous and the not-so-famous, have suffered at the hands of the press. But the one who has suffered misrepresentation more than most, and for longer than any, is Jesus. Many, many times the words of Jesus have been quoted (and misquoted!), analysed and interpreted in a variety of ways. Unfortunately, many of those interpretations are possible only because Jesus' words have been torn from their original context — just like the Archbishop's question.

The great debate

This has happened frequently over the years in that debate about Jesus to which scholars (and others) return with almost monotonous regularity: 'Who was Jesus?' Or should it be: 'Who *is* Jesus?' A good man? A fine teacher? A world-class religious leader? How far is it legitimate to suggest that he was more than a man, that he was in some sense divine? Is this what Christians mean when they call him the 'Son of God'? The debate has been endless. Of course, there have always been plenty of sceptics who dismiss as nonsense any talk of Jesus being divine. Sometimes they will add by way of a parting shot, 'Anyway, Jesus never said he was God!'

On the face of it, we have to admit that they are right: as far as we know Jesus never actually said, 'I am God!' So perhaps we have to concede that the sceptics are right.

It's not as easy as that, however. More careful examination of the life of Jesus reveals that many of the things he said and did, when understood against their historical background and cultural context, look much more like claims for divinity than perhaps seemed to be the case at first sight. It is the purpose of this book to show that in a variety of ways, and on many different occasions, Jesus did claim to be divine. Maybe he never did so directly, and at times it might seem somewhat obscure; but claim it he did, time after time after time. The evidence, I believe, is considerable and persuasive.

The basic text

Inevitably, it has been necessary to refer frequently to, and quote extensively from, the New Testament, especially the Gospels. I do so fully aware of the detailed scrutiny and analysis to which it has been subjected by scholars: I am aware of the questions that have been asked, the doubts that have been expressed, and the challenges to its trustworthiness that have been made.

But I am also aware of other scholarship which serves rather to support and affirm the New Testament. Archaeological research has identified buildings and places mentioned in the New Testament the existence of which had been doubted: it can be doubted no longer. Historians, particularly those specializing in Jewish and Roman history, have corroborated not only events described in the New Testament but many historical details referred to as well. Other experts have shown that the writings of the New Testament are clearly authentic, based on sources very close to the original events, and written within the lifetime of some who were contemporaries of Jesus. What is more, some of the existing manuscripts of the New Testament are very early indeed; there is a gap of only a few years between the original writing and copies that we have now, which allows very little room for corruption and misrepresentation.

In fact, the New Testament has stood the test of time and the attack of critics remarkably well. Many who have read it with an open mind have found that it 'rings true' — and even that is evidence which should not be dismissed too lightly.

Bearing all these things in mind, I am persuaded that we have in the New Testament a reliable account of the life and teaching of Jesus; so I use it as a basis for this book happily and without apology.

There is another important reason for quoting the text of the New Testament as much as I have. A generation ago, there was usually, even amongst those with only nominal Christian faith, some knowledge of Jesus, if only 'the stories of Jesus' remembered from Sunday-school days. Today that is not so. Increasingly, I find people have little or no knowledge of the life and teaching of Jesus, let alone any understanding of its significance. There are some who would even struggle to explain the significance of major Christian festivals such as Christmas and Easter.

So, the New Testament is quoted (with book, chapter and verse references such as Mark 4:35) by way of introducing people to the life and teaching of Jesus, hoping that some may have their appetites whetted by the snippets they read here, and will want to read it for themselves. In the end, that is a far better place to find out about Jesus.

1
'You don't know what you're talking about!'

Jesus went to the territory near the town of Caesarea Philippi, where he asked his disciples, 'Who do people say the Son of Man is?'

'Some say John the Baptist,' they answered. 'Others say Elijah, while others say Jeremiah or some other prophet.'

'What about you?' he asked them. 'Who do you say I am?'

Simon Peter answered, 'You are the Messiah, the Son of the living God.'

(Matthew 16:13–16)

How often have you been on the receiving end of unhelpful advice? Perhaps you never actually asked for it in the first place; and even if you did, it turned out to be useless, if not disastrous. Maybe it was mother-in-law with her amazing knowledge of everything from bathing the baby to asphalting the front drive. Or that irritating person who always seems to know how to live other people's lives better than they do — his advice usually begins, 'If I were you . . .' Or there is that friend who seems to have an opinion on everything under the sun — he's actually a bit of a bore. Have you ever wanted to say to such people (with a great deal of tact if it's your mother-in-law), 'You don't know what you're talking about!'?

Often, that is just what I feel like saying to people who talk

13

about Jesus. Many these days are ready to pass judgment on Jesus, to offer an opinion about him; the trouble is the things they say are often unfair and even way out. Of course, everyone is entitled to his own opinion and must be free to express it. But what if that opinion could not be supported by the facts? Imagine the chaos that would reign if a firm of civil engineers based their calculations on opinions rather than facts: how many of their bridges would stay up? Or what if an architect drew up his plans on the basis of opinion rather than fact? Architects and engineers must deal with facts: it would be foolish and dangerous to do otherwise.

Yet intelligent people often have firmly-held opinions about Jesus which show that they have never considered the facts, examined the evidence, or even read the documents which speak about him. Frequently they are embarrassed into silence by being asked: 'How long is it since you read a Gospel?' Time and again it would be appropriate to say to them: 'You don't know what you're talking about!'

One thing is certain: there is increasing interest today in the person of Jesus. Many have no time for the church, theology leaves them cold, and yet there is a strange fascination about Jesus. Such is the interest that when the six-hour-long film *Jesus of Nazareth* was shown on British television a few years ago, it enjoyed an estimated audience of 21 million (and 91 million saw it in the States).

But there is a problem: opinions differ. There are so many different ideas about Jesus that it's really rather confusing. It's enough to make you cry out in despair, 'Will the real Jesus please stand up!'

Opinions galore

If you have been to a performance of *Godspell*, then you will have seen Jesus portrayed as a rather zany clown. Certainly the show succeeded in communicating something of the excitement and joy which must have been a feature of the life and ministry of Jesus.

But was Jesus really like that?

Maybe you are one of the two million people who have enjoyed the record-breaking show *Jesus Christ Superstar*. There, Jesus is depicted as a kind of popular cult figure, the leader of an unremarkable and short-lived movement. In the end, what did he achieve? Any success he might have had was cut short by his death — and that was that!

Is that a fair assessment of the life of Jesus?

Perhaps you have been stopped in the street by the 'Moonies', members of the Unification Church. They have been active in many countries recently, giving out literature, collecting for 'missionary work', and organizing lectures to introduce people to their beliefs. They will talk about Jesus; they will tell you that he failed in his mission to bring the kingdom of heaven on earth. He should have married and raised a perfect family — his death on a cross was the final proof of his failure. Because he failed, a new Messiah is needed to continue and complete the work: he was born in Korea in 1920, the Reverend Sun Myung Moon.

Are they right?

Some, in recent years, have become fascinated by the mysticism of eastern religions. Sometimes Jesus features in their writings and beliefs, usually as a 'guru', God's representative on earth. But there have been many gurus, and Jesus has long since been superseded by newer, more up-to-date models.

Is that all that can be said for Jesus?

Even some of the other great world religions have considerable admiration for Jesus. Many Hindus, for example, think very highly of his teaching, in particular the Sermon on the Mount. It is significant that a recent box-office success in India was *Embodiment of Mercy*, a film about the life of Jesus made by a Hindu.

Similarly, Muslims respect Jesus and are happy to hail him as one of the world's great prophets. He is referred to on a number of occasions in their scriptures, the Quran, and such is the interest in him that 'Jesus people' within Islam are not an unknown phenomenon.

Jews, too, although they have rejected Jesus as their Messiah, and despite the unfortunate hostilities between Jews and Christians over the years, have never lost their interest in the person of Jesus. Jewish scholars have done some serious study of the New Testament, particularly the gospels, and have found much there to approve and affirm.

Most surprising of all, perhaps, is the enthusiasm of Marxists for Jesus. In one sense, it is not difficult to see why: Jesus often ended up clashing with the establishment, he frequently sided with the poor and the downtrodden, and he offered an attractive alternative society — he called it the kingdom of God. Marxists, of course, would want to leave God out of it; but in Jesus they find a revolutionary figure with much of whose radical, disturbing teaching they would agree.

Are Marxists the true followers of Jesus?

Who is Jesus?

So many opinions: whom do you believe?

Does any of them really know what he is talking about?

Who is Jesus?

What is Jesus?

A great man, a fine teacher of ethics, an outstanding religious leader, a remarkable prophet, a revolutionary — who is he?

No-one can seriously deny that Jesus lived: first-century historians, both Jewish and Roman, have settled that one — Jesus appears in their histories. Few would seriously challenge the fact that Jesus was a man, with a body rather like yours and mine. Many are happy to acknowledge that Jesus made an above-average impact on the world, not only in his own day but ever since.

The question is, can we, with any certainty, say any more

about Jesus than this? Is he in any sense unique? Is it reasonable to suggest that he might actually be divine? Christians claim that he is both unique and divine. Are they right?

Conflicting opinions about Jesus are nothing new: there were plenty flying around in Jesus' own day. The incident quoted at the beginning of this chapter illustrates that very clearly. Some people thought Jesus was the recently beheaded John the Baptist come back to life, others that he was Elijah; some reckoned he was Jeremiah, while others were not sure exactly who he was but thought he was probably one of the other Old Testament prophets. Then there was his disciple Peter's rather different opinion about Jesus: that he was the Messiah, the Son of the living God. Jesus reckoned that Peter's answer was the right one and commended him for it.

But was he right? If so, how did he arrive at his answer? Could it have been the things which Jesus said and did that led him to that conclusion?

Of course, Peter was actually there when it all happened. It is much harder for us, living nearly 2,000 years later, to observe Jesus in the way Peter was able to do. There have been many over the years who have spent their time (and earned their keep) studying the life and teaching of Jesus; they have produced vast numbers of books recording their discoveries. They are experts in the field and they ought to be able to help us find an answer to the question: 'Who is Jesus?'

Unfortunately, there are two problems: first, their books are also full of conflicting opinions about Jesus; secondly, they are often written in a language which is complicated and full of theological jargon. In fact, if we read too many of them we may end up more confused than when we started!

One student recognized this uncanny knack of theologians to complicate and confuse the issue and rewrote the incident in the life of Jesus which we have mentioned. It appeared as

17

graffiti on a wall in St John's University, New York, and reads:

> Jesus said to them, 'Who do you say that I am?'
>
> They replied, 'You are the eschatological manifestation of the ground of our being, the kerygma of which we find the ultimate meaning in our interpersonal relationships.'
>
> And Jesus said, 'What?'

(Nigel Rees, *Quote, Unquote*, Allen and Unwin, 1980)

Jesus' question to his disciples, 'Who do you say I am?', is a very important one, and deserves an honest, thoughtful, informed answer from each of us. We should not rely on uninformed opinion. So, let us listen to Jesus: let him speak for himself, and let us take careful note of all he has to say about himself. In other words, in order to answer Jesus' question, we are going to ask another: 'Who does he think he is?'

2
Just what you've been waiting for

Jesus was born in a stable. Now that is scarcely earth-shattering news: to many it is very familiar — our Christmas carols are full of references to the stable, and it is a favourite subject for Christmas-card artists.

Jesus was born in Bethlehem. That, too, is well known, if only because Bethlehem also features prominently in our Christmas carols. What is more, thousands of people, Christians and non-Christians alike, travel to that small Middle-Eastern town each year chiefly because it is the birthplace of Jesus.

Jesus was also born a Jew. Now that is less well known, or, at least, more often forgotten. Even those who know it often have not realized the significance of it. In fact, it is of great importance, more important than his birth either in a stable or in Bethlehem.

But why? Surely, if he is supposed to be the Saviour of the world, the man for all people, then it doesn't really matter where he was born, or what nationality he had? But the truth of the matter is that, wherever else he might have been born, he wasn't. He was born a Jew and we do well to remember that. Why? Because all of us are affected by our environment: our nationality, our education, the influences of our home, the attitudes of those around us. We can either accept these influences, or reject them, but one way or another they affect us.

And Jesus was no exception. He was born a Jew and brought up surrounded by Jewish ideas and attitudes — he could not escape them. So what? Does it matter? It does if we are to have any chance of understanding him; it matters if we want to answer his question 'Who do you say I am?' in an informed way; it matters if we are to pass judgment on Jesus without being accused of not knowing what we are talking about.

Putting Jesus in context

Jews have always had a strong national identity, the sense of belonging together. They are also justly proud of their nation's history and traditions which go back thousands of years. For them, too, religion is an integral part of their history, so that it is difficult to talk about their history without talking about their religion.

At the heart of this religion was the conviction that they had a very special part to play in God's plans: that he had chosen to reveal himself to them especially, and to make himself known to other nations through them — they were 'God's chosen people'.

Over the years, a number of individuals had had particularly significant roles to play. There was Abraham, for example, the founder of the nation and father of their faith; there was Moses who first set down their laws and beliefs; and there was a succession of 'prophets' who appeared at various times in their history to bring God's word of judgment, correction and instruction.

For the Jew, his chief point of reference for every aspect of life was the collection of writings (Scriptures) which had been gathered together over the years — our Old Testament. There was one particular idea, recurring right through these Scriptures, which was of supreme importance to them; that God would one day send a Deliverer who would set them free and establish the rule of God on earth in human affairs — the 'kingdom of God'. It was the promise of a 'Messiah', not just for them, but for all nations. To the coming of this special person they looked forward eagerly.

These, in brief, are the traditions Jesus inherited, in which he was brought up. This is the setting for all he said and did; this is the background against which his life and teaching must be understood.

The right time has come and the Kingdom of God is near!
Turn away from your sins and believe the Good News!
(Mark 1:15)

These striking words are possibly the first Jesus uttered in public. The uninitiated could well miss the significance of them; but those who were there, steeped in the same traditions as Jesus, would not have missed it. When Jesus spoke of 'the right time', he was referring to that time when God would act, fulfilling his promises, sending his Messiah, delivering his people, and inaugurating his kingdom. In effect, Jesus was saying, 'That moment for which you have been waiting so long has arrived.'

One Sabbath day not long after that, Jesus attended the synagogue in his home town of Nazareth. He was invited to read a lesson, and was handed the book (or rather, the scroll) containing the writings of one of their prophets, Isaiah. This is what he read:

The Spirit of the Lord is upon me,
    because he has chosen me to bring good news to the
    poor.
He has sent me to proclaim liberty to the captives
    and recovery of sight to the blind;
to set free the oppressed
    and announce that the time has come
    when the Lord will save his people (Luke 4:18-19).

When he had finished, Jesus handed the scroll back to the attendant and sat down. All eyes were on him now, because, according to synagogue tradition, if the reader sits down after the lesson it means he is going to preach, to explain the passage he has read.

They waited with more-than-usual attention, because Jesus was the 'local lad' who was gaining a reputation for himself as a somewhat unorthodox and highly provocative teacher. What would he have to say this morning?

What is more, the passage he had read was one of their favourites, one of the bits which speaks of God's Deliverer who is going to come.

There must have been a hushed expectancy in the synagogue that morning; not for a long time had they awaited the sermon with such interest.

We do not know all Jesus said; only the main thrust of his message has been recorded for us. But we have enough to know that the congregation must have been amazed and astonished at what they heard.

'This passage of scripture', Jesus said, 'has come true today, as you heard it being read' (Luke 4:21).

Could it be true, that the Messiah for whom they had been waiting for so long had arrived? Could Jesus, the local lad from Nazareth, really be God's deliverer? Was he going to liberate them?

One thing is certain, whatever the congregation thought that morning, the preacher seemed to be convinced that Isaiah's prophecy was being fulfilled: that he was God's chosen Servant, the Deliverer, the Messiah.

It was not just a few special passages of Scripture that Jesus claimed to fulfil. He believed that the whole of the Old Testament pointed to his coming, that wherever you looked you would find it speaking about him.

The religious leaders of Jesus' day were experts in interpreting the Scriptures — or so they reckoned. Jesus thought differently: he reckoned they were blind and resistant to truth. They studied the Scriptures but failed to see Jesus in them, and he scolded them for their failure: 'You study the Scriptures, because you think that in them you will find eternal life. And these very Scriptures speak about me! Yet you are not willing to come to me in order to have life' (John 5:39–40).

Arguing with religious leaders was a frequent part of Jesus' public life. Mind you, he did challenge them very directly, and they weren't going to take it lying down. 'If you obey my teaching, you are really my disciples; you will know the truth, and the truth will set you free.'

Now no-one was going to tell *them* they weren't free! 'We are the descendants of Abraham, and we have never been anybody's slaves.'

Presumably, by referring to Abraham, their great forefather, they were hoping to strengthen their case. But Jesus was totally unimpressed.

'If you really were Abraham's children, you would do the same things that he did . . . You are trying to kill me. Abraham did nothing like this!'

That's telling them! And there was more to come. 'I am telling you the truth: whoever obeys my teaching will never die.'

That was just too much for them: 'Now we are certain that you have a demon! Abraham died, and the prophets died, yet you say that whoever obeys your teaching will never die. Our father Abraham died; you do not claim to be greater than Abraham, do you? And the prophets also died. Who do you think you are?'

What a question to ask Jesus! That was exactly what he was claiming to be: greater than their greatest forefather, Abraham. And he told them so. Is it any wonder that the conversation ended with an attempt on Jesus' life? (John 8:31–59).

These religious leaders also looked to Moses, the great Old Testament lawgiver, as an authority in matters of belief and behaviour. Again they claimed to be experts in the field. Unfortunately, as Jesus was quick to point out, some parts of Moses' writings they conveniently ignored, and their understanding of other parts was decidedly questionable. Most serious of all, they failed to see any reference to Jesus in Moses' writings.

'If you had really believed Moses, you would have

believed me, because he wrote about me. But since you do not believe what he wrote, how can you believe what I say?' (John 5:46–47).

Whether Jesus was referring to a particular part of Moses' writings or simply to the general drift of his teaching we can only guess. Certainly, Moses did speak of the coming of 'a prophet like me from among your own people' (Deuteronomy 18:15), and Jesus may have had that in mind as he spoke. Understandably, such comments did not endear him to his religious opponents; according to them, claims like these were dangerous, outrageous, and, worst of all, blasphemous — and so they were unless they were true!

Whatever his contemporaries thought about him, one thing is clear: Jesus believed himself to be the climax of history thus far, the culmination of the long historical and religious tradition of the Jewish nation. Because he believed that, he made some alarming claims about himself: that he was greater than Abraham, the founder of the nation; that Moses, their lawgiver, wrote about him; that he was the fulfilment of all their Scriptures. Above all, he claimed to be the specially chosen and appointed Servant of God, the promised Deliverer of God's people, the long-awaited Messiah.

It should be no surprise, therefore, that when he asked his disciples the question, 'Who do you say I am?', he applauded Peter for his answer: 'You are the Messiah.'

And that is why Christians call Jesus of Nazareth 'Christ' (which means the same as Messiah). It is not a title he was given by his early followers, or one dreamt up by later scholars, but it is one he claimed for himself.

Claims of this kind, made by Jesus about himself, should not be overlooked by anyone wanting to answer in an informed way Jesus' still-pertinent question: 'Who do you say I am?'

3
Father and I

'He's got a thing about it!' 'He's a fanatic!'

In this rather scathing way we sometimes dismiss anyone who has an absorbing interest which seems to take up most of their time, money and energy. They are always doing 'it', always talking about 'it', whether it's girls, or sport, or trains, or music, or whatever else.

Jesus, you might have said, was a fanatic. He was always talking about God. That in itself is not really surprising, since he was one of the world's great religious leaders and teachers. In fact, it would be strange if he did not talk about God.

The surprising thing is not that Jesus talked about God, or even that he talked about him as much as he did, but rather the *way* he talked about him, and, in particular, the way he talked about his own relationship to him. Consider this, for example: 'My Father has given me all things. No one knows the Son except the Father, and no one knows the Father except the Son and those to whom the Son chooses to reveal him' (Matthew 11:27).

If you take these words at their face value (and that is usually the best way to understand the words of Jesus recorded in the Gospels), it sounds as if Jesus is claiming a rather special kind of relationship between himself (the Son) and God (the Father). In fact this relationship is more than special: it is all-but exclusive.

Time and again, Jesus spoke in this exclusive way about God and about his relationship with God. Often, he would repeat his claim in this way: 'I have come from the Father', or 'The Father has sent me.'

That kind of talk is dangerous, unless you are absolutely sure you are right.

Certainly it invites opposition, and Jesus has had plenty of that. He is possibly the most controversial individual ever to walk this earth. But then, he had the habit of saying the most outrageous things at times. For example: 'I am the way, the truth, and the life; no one goes to the Father except by me' (John 14:6).

One way

These words of Jesus prove to be a problem whenever Christians talk with non-Christians, particularly today when it is considered right to be tolerant of the views of others. The problem is this: if Jesus is right that no-one can come to God except through him, then the common, 'tolerant' belief that there are many routes to God (rather like paths up a mountain), of which Jesus is just one, looks very shaky.

Of course, we could say Jesus did not really mean what he said; or we could conveniently forget that he said it. Some Bible scholars offer us a let-out by suggesting that these are words the Gospel-writer put on the lips of Jesus, rather than actual words spoken by Jesus. But, as we have already seen, there is rather more integrity about the New Testament than that. In any case, we must be very careful not to dismiss this or any other saying of Jesus simply because it is difficult to accommodate into our thinking.

The alternative is not easy. It means accepting the words of Jesus and standing by them. We then risk being accused of intolerance and arrogance: because here, Jesus is provocatively claiming to enjoy some kind of exclusive access to God and relationship with God. It is so exclusive, in fact, that if anyone else wants to come to God, they can do so only through Jesus — that is, anyone who wants to get to know God needs to get involved with Jesus.

26

Intimate

So close was Jesus' relationship with God that the name by which he called him most naturally was 'Father'. In fact, Jesus actually called God, in his native language Aramaic, 'Abba'. And that is remarkable, because 'Abba' is an expression of familiarity and intimacy such as a child would use of its father — indeed, in certain parts of the Middle East, children can still be heard today calling their fathers 'Abba'. It is almost as familiar as the English expressions 'Daddy' or 'Dad'.

What's so important about that?

Simply this: that religious people of Jesus' day took God very seriously indeed; they considered him great and powerful and holy, and therefore virtually unapproachable. They avoided calling him by name if they could, and when they did (in worship or prayer, for example) they would be very careful to use titles which conveyed proper respect and reverence for him. To call him 'Father', let alone 'Daddy', would have seemed thoroughly disrespectful and therefore unthinkable. The fact that Jesus did so repeatedly must have annoyed and upset many of his fellow Jews.

What is more, if you study the religions of the world, you will find very many different names and titles for God; but nowhere will you find anything comparable to the intimacy of 'Abba'. No other religious teacher has dared to use such a familiar way of addressing God. Yet Jesus even encouraged his followers to address God in the same intimate way, and they have done so ever since.

This is not only remarkable, it is unique.

Involved

Now if any ordinary person spoke constantly in this kind of way, most of us would find him insufferable. He would probably be somewhat aloof, regarding his fellow human beings with contempt and making many of us feel inferior and inadequate. The fascinating thing is that this is not the case with Jesus: there is no hint of superiority in his attitude to people at all, no trace of aloofness in his manner, no attempt to make anyone feel inadequate. On the contrary, he is open and welcoming to all, whoever they are; he has time for anyone who needs him, and no-one is too insignificant for him to bother with.

Take the blind beggar who was sitting in the gutter the day Jesus visited Jericho (Mark 10:46–52). When he heard that Jesus was passing he cried out to him. The people in the crowd told him to shut up and kicked him back in the gutter; but Jesus stopped, called the man to him, talked with him, and healed him. The crowd looked with contempt on him; Jesus looked with compassion on him.

There were those who suffered with leprosy. They were total outcasts from society. No-one would come anywhere near them for fear of catching their dreadful disease, and they were forced to live together away from everyone else. Imagine their amazement and excitement, therefore, when Jesus stopped to talk with them, was prepared to come near to them, and, what is more, actually touched them (Mark 1:40–42). No-one else would, but Jesus did.

On another occasion, religious people brought to Jesus a woman who had been caught committing adultery. Actually, the men who brought her were much more concerned about getting Jesus to incriminate himself by putting him on the spot, than ever they were about the woman and her needs. They were ready to throw the book at her, and the book said that the punishment for adultery was death by stoning. What would Jesus say? In his book, things like love and forgiveness were written large, and, although he could not condone her sin, he was willing to love and forgive even this immoral woman (John 8:1–11).

So, being careful not to fall into the trap set for him by flouting the Jewish law, Jesus suggested that the one of her accusers who was without sin should throw the first stone. No wonder they all slunk away one by one and left her alone with Jesus. Her accusers were full of self-righteous contempt for her; Jesus was full of self-effacing compassion.

Tax-collectors were also despised members of the community. Perhaps you're not too fond of your tax-collector; things were worse in Jesus' day. To begin with, they were employed by the foreign occupying power; but also, they were poorly paid, and they usually overcharged their clients to make up for it. No wonder people didn't rush to count them amongst their friends.

But all that didn't bother Jesus too much. He had a former tax-collector amongst his closest friends (Matthew 9:9), he spent the night in the home of another (Luke 19:1–10), and often had meals with them.

The religious people couldn't understand it. Any self-respecting teacher ought to know all about these sinful people and steer well clear of them. Jesus' critics were puzzled and annoyed that he didn't seem to agree. Consequently, he was frequently criticized for the company he kept, and was eventually dubbed 'the friend of sinners'. It was meant to be a term of abuse; I suspect Jesus welcomed it, possibly more than any other title.

When we put the words and actions of Jesus alongside each other like this, we are confronted with a striking contrast; teaching which claims exclusive relationship with God, and a life which is totally involved with human beings.

How do we reconcile these things?

How do *you* answer Jesus' question: 'Who do you say I am?'

4
Man and God?

There are some people who have the marvellous ability to tell a good story well. They are both captivating and convincing. The trouble is they can be too convincing, leaving you struggling to separate fact from fiction, believing what is only a story and doubting what is true.

There are those who have that kind of difficulty with Jesus: trying to distinguish fact from fiction in his teaching. Often they will make from his teaching a selection which they have decided is true, and dismiss the rest as 'just nice stories'. The trouble with such a selection is that it is inevitably both subjective and arbitrary, and therefore probably misleading. It would be better either to accept or to reject all Jesus' teaching.

Of course, accepting it has its problems, as we have seen – it certainly stretches the mind! We have already considered Jesus' provocative claims to have exclusive access to God, and to have the right to call God 'Father'. To claim any more than that would surely be stretching the point just too far: in any case, it must be impossible without actually claiming to be God's equal. Yet, Jesus had the audacity to do just that: openly to declare himself God's equal — or so it appears.

Remember that argument about Abraham in chapter 2? Those religious leaders were none too pleased with Jesus' claim to be greater than Abraham: in fact, they were furious and angrily asked him: 'Who do you think you are, saying things like that?' (Their actual words were: 'You are not even fifty years old — and you have seen Abraham?' [John 8:57] — but it amounts to the same thing.)

That was the cue for Jesus to play his trump card and win the game: 'I am telling you the truth. Before Abraham was born, "I Am".'

Even if the grammar is a bit unusual, Jesus' answer sounds harmless enough, and you may wonder why it produced the violent reaction it did.

'I am'

It all began in the time of Moses, their other great national hero. When God called on him to lead the Israelites out of slavery in Egypt, Moses was reluctant to accept — in fact, he played hard to get. (You can read about it in Exodus 3.) He offered all sorts of excuses for not going. One of the more reasonable was that he couldn't explain who had sent him. 'God, they will want to know who sent me. What do I tell them? What is your name?' God replied (and it's a little difficult to make it sound sense in English): 'I am who I am.' And he added: 'This is what you must say to them: "The one who is called I AM has sent me to you".'

Clearly, Jesus' use of the phrase 'I am' would remind his hearers of that incident and of that special name for God. More than that, the fact that Jesus said, 'Before Abraham was born, I *am*', and not 'I *was*', would suggest something else: that he was claiming to be what only God really is, eternal. Only God can legitimately claim 'I am' at any time, past, present, or future; but there is Jesus saying that he is also eternal: that his birth in Bethlehem was not his beginning, that he had always been in existence, even before Abraham.

This was highly provocative. Jesus must have realized that his words would imply these things and would arouse the anger of his critics. By applying the name 'I am' to himself, Jesus was taking for himself something that was properly God's alone: he was claiming to be God's equal. One

31

commentator on this incident has remarked: 'These are the words of the most impudent blasphemer that ever spoke, or the words of God incarnate.'

His critics took it as blasphemy, and, in their book, the punishment for that was death by stoning. So angry were they by now, that they dispensed with arrest, trial and sentence, grabbed the nearest stones, and took pot-shots at him there and then.

The same as God?

On another occasion, Jesus was minding his own business in the temple at Jerusalem when a crowd began to gather. Just like famous people today, Jesus found it hard to escape the crowds. They started asking awkward questions, of which the most direct was, 'Tell us the plain truth: are you the Messiah?' (John 10:22–24). Jesus' reply was unexpected: 'The Father and I are one' (John 10:30). Could he possibly mean it?

There are many religious groups and sects around today (Mormons and Jehovah's Witnesses to name just two) who will tell you that all Jesus meant when he said this was that he shared with God the same aims, desires and goals; that their hearts and minds were united; that they had a common mission. If that were so, Jesus' reply is harmless: it would certainly be unfair to accuse him of blasphemy. Yet, apparently, those who were present thought otherwise. To their ears, Jesus was again declaring himself God's equal, and that was blasphemy. And so, as before, dispensing with the legal formalities, they tried to stone him on the spot (John 10:31).

Even Jesus' own close friends were slow to grasp exactly what he was saying. 'Lord, show us the Father; that is all we need,' Philip asked him after being with him for nearly three years.

Jesus' answer was tinged with sadness, but was nevertheless direct: 'For a long time I have been with you all; yet you do not know me, Philip? Whoever has seen me has

32

seen the Father. Why, then, do you say, "Show us the Father"? Do you not believe, Philip, that I am in the Father and the Father is in me?' (John 14:8–10).

It was just as well that Jesus was alone with his disciples, and that none of his opponents was around to chuck stones at him. Undoubtedly, they would have obliged if they had been within earshot: for here was the same outrageous and 'blasphemous' claim again, that Jesus was God's equal.

Clearly, Jesus believed that it was not simply that he had exclusive access to God, nor even that he enjoyed a specially intimate relationship with God, but that he was actually God's equal — he was God.

A real man
But that is not the complete picture.

As we saw before, if, alongside the claims of Jesus, we examine the life of Jesus, we find a fascinating contrast. To be God's equal is to be more than human. Yet, in his life, he appears to be very much an ordinary man, displaying thoroughly human characteristics and behaviour.

There was the time, for example, when children were brought to him for blessing. The disciples tried to send them away (perhaps they had had an exhausting day), but Jesus welcomed them, took them in his arms, and blessed them (Mark 10:13–16). And on another occasion, when the disciples asked him who was the greatest in the kingdom of heaven, he replied by taking a child as a visual aid and saying: 'Unless you change and become like children, you will never enter the Kingdom of heaven' (Matthew 18:1–5).

Not only did he enjoy natural human activities such as the company of children, he also knew the same physical weaknesses that we all know so well. We find him tired out on a journey and resting for a while by a well (John 4:5–6); he was hungry after going without food for forty days (Matthew 4:2), and thirsty as he hung dying on the cross (John 19:28); he became exhausted by a long programme of preaching and teaching — on one occasion he actually fell asleep in the back of a boat, and managed to sleep through a violent storm (Mark 4:35-38).

He experienced every human emotion, too. He knew the joy of celebration and was happy to be a guest at a wedding (John 2:1-11); he knew the sadness of losing a close friend, and was prepared to weep openly at his grave (John 11:33-36). He felt great compassion for people in their need, whether it was for a crowd 'because they were like sheep without a shepherd' (Mark 6:34), or for an individual such as the rich man whose wealth kept him from finding eternal life — we are told that Jesus looked at him and loved him (Mark 10:21).

Both/and

Jesus was a man all right — it's hard to deny that, looking at his life. But what of his claims to be God? Can he actually be both?

The first followers of Jesus certainly seemed to think so. Two of the Gospel writers said so explicitly in their accounts of the birth of Jesus.

Luke records the visit of an angel to Mary telling her that she would become pregnant and give birth to a son. Since she was then unmarried, she was understandably alarmed and asked how it could happen. The angel replied: 'The Holy Spirit will come on you, and God's power will rest upon you. For this reason the holy child will be called the Son of God' (Luke 1:26-35).

Matthew highlights the experience of Joseph, Mary's fiancé. Joseph was understandably concerned when he discovered she was pregnant and he contemplated calling off the engagement. But God spoke to him and reassured him: 'Do not be afraid to take Mary to be your wife. For it is by the Holy Spirit that she has conceived' (Matthew 1:18-25).

This part of the Gospel account, possibly more than any other, is difficult for some to accept — it sounds more like fantasy than fact. Yet it is entirely consistent with the rest of the Gospel accounts, and it provides an explanation of that contrast between the divine claims and human life of Jesus.

34

Both Matthew and Luke tell us that Jesus was born of Mary and is therefore man, but was conceived by the Spirit of God and is therefore God. And that is precisely what Christians have believed down the centuries. It is concisely expressed in the Apostles' Creed, one of the earliest statements of Christian belief, still used regularly in worship by many Christians: 'I believe in Jesus Christ . . . He was conceived by the power of the Holy Spirit and born of the Virgin Mary.'

To say that Jesus is both man and God is neither to twist the evidence, nor to dismiss part of it, but rather to face up realistically to the whole of it.

But you must examine the evidence yourself.

'Who do *you* say I am?'

5
Truth or arrogance?

There are some people (maybe you know one or two) who always seem to be full of themselves, singing their own praises, full of their own importance — God's gift to the human race, so they think. They are not usually the easiest of people to get on with.

At first sight, Jesus appears to be a bit like that; certainly he talks a lot about himself and seems to offer himself to others as the answer to their needs. The important question we need to ask, of course, is: 'Does he have any right to talk this way?'

What about this, for example: 'I am the light of the world' (John 8:12)? That is a strange thing for anyone to say. In what possible way can one man be the source of light for the whole world? And is he implying by this that apart from him and without him people are, in effect, in darkness? That would certainly seem to be the case, for he goes on: 'Whoever follows me will have the light of life and will never walk in darkness.' As if to underline it, he repeats it: 'I have come into the world as light, so that everyone who believes in me should not remain in the darkness' (John 12:46). Follow me, believe in me, says Jesus, because without me you will simply grope and stumble your way through life, risking making wrong decisions and going in the wrong direction – without me it will be like walking in the dark.

Unless it is true, that's arrogant talk. And for those who were there when he said it, it was made worse because they would detect in these words a subtle claim to be divine. For them, 'light' was a description of God himself, and the only one who had the right to claim to be the light of the world was God. So Jesus' claim was daring indeed: he claimed to be what God alone is supposed to be, and therefore claimed to offer people light which would make a radical difference to their lives.

An offer of life . . .

There were many in Jesus' day who found life hard, who had become disillusioned and dissatisfied and were looking for something better, more fulfilling. There are many like that in our society too. Today various agencies exist which offer help, advice and support to such people: the doctor may prescribe drugs, the psychiatrist may advise a course of counselling, the social worker may recommend involvement in some community project. Of course, none of these was available in Jesus' day, but, even so, his advice to some of the needy people he met was surprising, to say the least.

Take, for example, the Samaritan woman he met when he stopped by a well to rest on a journey (John 4). The fact that she had come alone to draw water in the middle of the day suggests that all was not well: gathering water was normally an early-morning, communal activity. It becomes apparent that her problem was a moral one, involving men. But Jesus, with his keen perception, realized that her real problem was much deeper; so he said to her, 'Whoever drinks this water will be thirsty again, but whoever drinks the water that I will give him will never be thirsty again. The water that I will give will become in him a spring which will provide him with life-giving water and give him eternal life' (verses 13–14).

Understandably, the woman didn't really comprehend what Jesus meant: she thought he was talking about actual water. In fact, he was addressing himself to her real problem which was not a thirst for water, nor even a thirst for sex, but

37

a thirst for life. But before she could begin to enjoy that life, Jesus had to help her see what she was really like, and challenge her to change her ways. So he asked her to fetch her husband — and then the truth was out. She had been married to five men, but the man with whom she was now living was not really her husband (verses 17–18).

For a while she struggled with Jesus' offer of life-giving water and its implications for her, but gradually she was released and was able to receive that offer. As a result, she was transformed and immediately began to bring others to Jesus, whom she now realized was 'the Saviour of the world' (verse 42).

. . . for the dissatisfied

Here and elsewhere Jesus spoke of his offer in terms of life-giving water. What exactly did he mean? There is a clue in something he said a little later: 'Whoever is thirsty should come to me and drink' (John 7:37).

Could he mean us to drink him? That is what he seems to be saying, especially when he changes the metaphor from water to bread: 'I am the living bread that came down from heaven. If anyone eats this bread, he will live for ever' (John 6:51).

How do you eat and drink Jesus? He explained: 'I am the bread of life. He who comes to me will never be hungry; he who believes in me will never be thirsty' (John 6:35).

To those who are dissatisfied and unfulfilled in life (for that is surely what the imagery of hunger and thirst is meant to convey) Jesus offers himself. The impact of this would have been greater still to his contemporaries because for them, more than for us, bread and water represented the absolute necessities of life.

Jesus' message therefore is that he is essential for life: without him there will be frustration, restlessness and emptiness, with him there will be fulfilment. To come to Jesus, to believe in Jesus, to eat and drink Jesus, is to discover life at its best. 'I have come', said Jesus, 'in order that you might have life – life in all its fullness' (John 10:10).

And that message Jesus repeated on numerous occasions and in different ways: for any who find life a problem for any reason, Jesus is the answer. 'Come to me, all of you who are tired from carrying heavy loads, and I will give you rest' (Matthew 11:28).

But lest we get the impression that it is simply a case of coming to Jesus with our problems and having them solved, he added: 'Take my yoke and put it on you, and learn from me, because I am gentle and humble in spirit; and you will find rest' (Matthew 11:29).

In other words, there are strings attached to Jesus' offer, as the Samaritan woman discovered: if we would come to Jesus for relief, if we would receive his offer of life, then we need to respond by living our lives in harness with his, yoked to him — that means living for him, not for ourselves.

. . . for the self-assured

Of course, we are not all inadequates, social misfits or moral deviants, we don't all have 'problems' or 'hang-ups'. Some of us are actually remarkably balanced, confident, fulfilled, and even moral individuals — even if we do say it ourselves. Does Jesus have anything to say to us?

In fact, Jesus frequently met people who were every bit as self-assured as many of us; some of the things he said must have shocked and surprised them.

There was Nicodemus, for example, a leader in the community: he was well-educated, well-connected, well-respected, and devoutly religious. Concerned for his reputation, he approached Jesus under cover of night (John 3). Jesus' reputation had reached him and he was fascinated by what he had heard; he wanted the opportunity to ask Jesus one or two searching religious questions. Jesus' response took him by surprise: 'I am telling you the truth: no one can see the Kingdom of God unless he is born again' (verse 3).

Now that didn't make a lot of sense, and Nicodemus argued about the impossibility of climbing back into his mother's womb and being born again. In fact, Nicodemus had misunderstood Jesus in the same way as the Samaritan woman had done: he was thinking physically, Jesus was speaking spiritually. Jesus saw that Nicodemus' real need was the same as the woman's: real spiritual life. This time, however, Jesus used a different imagery to make his point: he spoke of the need of a spiritual birth. However successful Nicodemus may have been, it could never bring him real life.

As far as we know, Nicodemus responded positively to Jesus' radical demand, unlike another young man he met. He also came asking questions (Mark 10:17–22): 'Good Teacher, what must I do to receive eternal life?'

Jesus reminded him of the ten commandments; he claimed that he had always kept them — and who knows, maybe he had. But Jesus knew the man's heart and realized what his real problem was. If he was to enjoy this eternal life he had asked about, then he would have to follow Jesus; in order to do that, he had to sell all his possessions. That was not something that all would-be followers of Jesus had to do necessarily, but it was necessary for this young man, because his problem was materialism — he loved things too much really to enjoy Jesus' offer of life. He had to choose. Sadly, Jesus' demand was just too much: 'Gloom spread over his face,' we are told, 'and he went away sad, because he was very rich' (verse 22).

To successful and needy alike, Jesus offered life — but on his terms. Often, the needy found his terms easier to accept than the successful.

. . . in the face of death
Successful or needy, there is one thing that comes to all eventually, and treats everyone exactly the same: death. Jesus had some surprising things to say on that subject too.

One day he was summoned to the home of some friends (John 11). The brother in the family, Lazarus, had become ill. By the time Jesus arrived he had died and was already buried. Try to imagine the scene: much grief, flowing tears, friends and family comforting one another over the loss of one they had loved dearly. Into that situation Jesus comes: he shares their sadness, sympathizes with them, and even weeps with them at the grave. But he also speaks to them of resurrection: 'Your brother will rise to life.'

That was fair enough: the family had some sort of belief that at the end of time those who had died would rise to life. But Jesus went on to say something new and surprising: 'I am the resurrection and the life. Whoever believes in me will live, even though he dies; and whoever lives and believes in me will never die' (verses 25–26).

We have already seen Jesus' claim to be the secret to fullness of life. Now he is claiming that this life is good beyond death too. What an exciting thing to say, if it's true!

So many people, both then and now, are afraid of death. It's the great unknown which is better not talked about. Some are so afraid of death that life now is spoiled for them. In the face of this real fear, Jesus offers life not just for now but for ever, not just until death but beyond death too — to believe in Jesus results in life which is untouched by death, what Jesus called 'eternal life'.

One follower of Jesus got the message: Jesus 'set free those who were slaves all their lives because of their fear of death' (Hebrews 2:15). That's good news, and it's highly relevant today. But is it true?

There's no getting away from it: Jesus claims to be the answer to the deepest needs of all people, both successful and needy, both in this life and in the life to come. He sums it all up like this: 'I am the way, the truth, and the life' (John 14:6).

Many have offered to others their advice: 'Go that way' or 'This is the way'. Jesus alone says, 'I am the way.' Wise teachers have often helped people discern good from evil, truth from error. Jesus alone says, 'I am the truth.' There has been no shortage of suggestions as to how to live well, how to get the most out of life. Jesus alone says, 'I am the life.'

No other way but Jesus? No truth outside Jesus? No life apart from Jesus? Did he really mean that?

. . . with strings attached

There is another aspect of all this which we have already begun to discover: that there are strings attached to Jesus' offer.

He makes it very clear that to benefit fully from what he offers, we have to be prepared to commit ourselves wholeheartedly to him — he demands to be first in our lives. 'If anyone wants to come with me, he must forget self, take up his cross every day, and follow me. For whoever wants to save his own life will lose it, but whoever loses his life for my sake will save it' (Luke 9:23–24). What right has anyone to expect another to lose his life for him?

Again, he says: 'Whoever comes to me cannot be my disciple unless he loves me more than he loves his father and his mother, his wife and his children, his brothers and his sisters, and himself as well' (Luke 14:26). How is that supposed to be reconciled with the commandment of God which says: 'Honour your father and your mother'? Clearly, Jesus is wanting first claim on our lives — no other relationship or friendship must be allowed to challenge that claim.

'None of you can be my disciple unless he gives up everything he has' (Luke 14:33). Does that mean that all followers of Jesus have to be homeless, friendless and penniless? They are certainly required to make everything else subordinate to following Jesus. Who *does* he think he is?

Truth or arrogance? Before we answer, we would do well to glance again at Jesus' life. Was it marked by selfishness and a struggle to control people? Not at all; in fact, the

42

opposite is true: he lived an utterly selfless life. He was always giving himself for others, teaching, healing, meeting people's needs. The demands made on him were enormous, and yet he always responded willingly, serving people whoever they were, however inconvenient. There were times when he tried to escape from the pressure for a while with his disciples, but crowds pursued them (Mark 3:7–8); even at home he was not left alone, so much so that, at times, Jesus and his friends had no time even to eat (Mark 3:20). When he was not serving people publicly he was praying for them privately, often getting up before dawn to get alone to pray (Mark 1:35). Even then he was not always left in peace, but people would search for him (Luke 4:42).

Never has there been a man who committed himself so completely to others, constantly giving himself to others regardless of the cost to himself, and, in the end, dying for the sake of others.

Somehow, Jesus' utter selflessness, rather than denying his demanding teaching, seems to give it credibility, urging us to the conclusion that if this is not arrogance (which it clearly is not), then it has to be truth. And if it is truth, then all his claims are valid, all his demands reasonable.

But what do you think? 'Who do you say I am?'

6
Who does he think he is ?

If anything is designed to make us rebel it is being told what to do. There is something in human nature which makes us resent being bossed around: we don't mind being *asked* to do something; we might even *volunteer* to do it; but being *told* we must do it is a different matter. Whether it's parents with children, or teachers with pupils, or bosses with workers, the same is true. It is worse still if someone comes in from outside, maybe to live near us or to work with us, and starts throwing his weight around, telling us what we should be doing and how to do it. We would very quickly tell him where to get off. After all, who does he think he is coming in here and telling us how to live our lives?

Jesus was for ever telling others what to think, and what to do, and how to live their lives.

Those who found it hardest to take were those who had known him from the start. To them, he was the local lad from Nazareth: they knew his mum and dad, they knew his home and family, they knew the carpenter's shop where he had learned his father's trade. No wonder they were puzzled when he began to preach and teach: they didn't know quite what to make of him.

Where on earth did he get all his ideas from, and that boldness and authority with which he spoke? He taught with such assurance and certainty: it was quite unnerving from such a young man. The things he said were so incredible that

44

anyone would have thought that he had been very well educated; and yet they knew he had had no special schooling, and he had certainly never been away to college.

They were astonished, perplexed, and just a bit uneasy. 'Isn't he the carpenter's son? Isn't Mary his mother, and aren't James, Joseph, Simon and Judas his brothers? Aren't all his sisters living here? Where did he get all this?' Uncomfortable and feeling threatened, they rejected him (Matthew 13:55–57).

Something different

But it was not only the people from his home town who recognized his wisdom and authority: many others did too. Wherever he went the crowds followed, and whenever he preached they would listen intently and want to hear more. There was something different about this teacher. They ought to know because there were so many religious teachers around, and they were used to listening to them.

They were familiar with their teaching method too: it usually consisted in referring to the thoughts and teachings of others, quoting first one great teacher and then another. Rarely did they offer their own thoughts or have anything original to say.

But the teaching of Jesus was very different and highly original. He apparently had little time for those other great teachers — at least, he didn't quote them anything like as freely and frequently as the other teachers did. Instead, he offered his own understanding of God, his own insight into religious affairs. He was prepared to pitch his authority against that of the scholars and teachers of the past. 'You have heard that it was said . . . But now I tell you . . .' was the bold way he taught the people. 'I am telling you the truth . . .' he would often say. 'I assure you' or 'Therefore I tell you' would frequently punctuate his preaching.

The people had never heard anything like it before: this was a new kind of teaching. 'When Jesus finished saying these things, the crowd was amazed at the way he taught. He wasn't like the teachers of the Law; instead, he taught with

45

authority' (Matthew 7:28-29). They were no fools: they recognized the difference all right. The Rabbis taught them from 'authorities'; Jesus taught them with authority — and they knew which rang true.

Miracles

His teaching was remarkable enough, but there was more to Jesus than that. Some of the things he *did* were unbelievable, enough to make people's eyes pop out of their heads and leave them open-mouthed in amazement. (There are those who still think they are unbelievable today and who therefore try to explain them away!)

There was the man with a dreadful skin-disease: Jesus touched him and he was healed. There was the man with a paralysed hand: Jesus told him to stretch out his useless hand and he did, and was healed. A man who was deaf and virtually dumb was brought to Jesus: he went away hearing and speaking without any impediment. A blind beggar was brought to Jesus and had his sight restored (Mark 1:40-45; 3:1-6; 7:31-35; 10:46-52). And there are many, many more: 'Everywhere Jesus went, to villages, towns, or farms, people would take those who were ill to the market places and beg him to let them at least touch the edge of his cloak; and all who touched it were made well' (Mark 6:56).

The reaction of the crowd to all this was predictable: they were amazed. 'All who heard were completely amazed. "How well he does everything!" they exclaimed. "He even causes the deaf to hear and the dumb to speak!"' (Mark 7:37).

Even death didn't defeat him: he was able to restore to life those who had died (Mark 5:21-43; Luke 7:11-16). There were other inexplicable things too: like the day when Jesus had been preaching to a large crowd (over 5,000) and then, on the spur of the moment, decided to offer them all supper. The trouble was that the only food they could find among that vast crowd was one young lad's packed lunch. Undeterred, Jesus took the boy's food, sat the people down, and then, after saying grace, actually managed to feed them all — and there was food left over (John 6:1-15)!

There was something uncanny about this man Jesus; there was in him some power which gave him this remarkable authority both in word and action. Even the elements seemed to respect his authority, judging by what happened one day on the Sea of Galilee.

Jesus was travelling by boat with his disciples; he was tired and had fallen asleep in the back of the boat. A storm blew up unexpectedly (which often happens on the Sea of Galilee because of the lie of the land). The disciples panicked and woke Jesus up. He calmly told the wind and waves to die down — and they did. That left the disciples wondering, 'Who is this man? Even the wind and the waves obey him!' (Mark 4:35-41).

Evil spiritual powers met their match in Jesus too. People were well aware of the dreadful effect evil could have on them, how it could possess them and destroy them; but rarely did they see that evil power resisted and defeated and its victims set free.

In Jesus they did.

He met a number of people who had been influenced and horribly spoiled by evil. Jesus faced up to them, spoke to the evil power just as he would address a person, and commanded its destructive work to cease. As the crowds watched, they saw these people released and transformed, becoming normal, rational human beings in a moment. They had never seen anything like it. 'The people were all so amazed that they started saying to one another, "What is this? Is it some kind of new teaching? This man has authority to give orders to the evil spirits, and they obey him!"' (Mark 1:27).

Authority

Here was a man with real authority: it was apparent in his teaching, visible in the miracles he did, unmistakable in his control of the elements, and supremely displayed in his challenge and defeat of evil. He had the power to command the attention of all: he would say to someone 'Come' and he came, to another 'Go' and he went, to another 'Follow me' and he did.

There was something about him that caused hardened fishermen and scheming tax-collectors to respond to his words, and, apparently, to drop everything and follow him (Mark 1:14–20; Luke 19:1–10).

But Jesus' authoritative manner got him into trouble — especially with religious people.

Like the day he was preaching in a house in Capernaum, packed to the doors with people eager to hear him. A paralysed man was brought by his friends and lowered through the roof to the feet of Jesus. Everyone could see what was wrong with him. Surely Jesus would heal him. To their surprise, and the anger of the religious leaders, Jesus looked at him and said, 'Your sins are forgiven.'

That was too much. Jesus may have authority, but one thing is certain: there is only one person with the authority to forgive a man his sins, and that is God. 'Who does he think he is, talking in this way? What right has he to say such things? This is blasphemy!'

Jesus' response was unexpected and direct: 'I will prove to you that the Son of Man has authority on earth to forgive sins.' With that, he turned to the sick man and told him to get up and go home; and he did (Mark 2:1–12).

What a man! He actually dared to do what God alone is supposed to do! If that is not a claim to be God, then what is?

Humility
Those who spend their time telling others what to do often treat people almost as their servants. Not so Jesus. Although he spoke and acted with authority, he lived in humility. He actually told his disciples that he had come not to be served, but to serve (Matthew 20:28).

When they ended up arguing about who was the greatest, Jesus reprimanded them: 'Whoever wants to be first must place himself last of all and be the servant of all' (Mark 9:33–35).

This must have sounded strange teaching to his contemporaries, radically different from the usual line on greatness. What is more, with Jesus it was more than words: he practised what he preached, supremely on the occasion of the last meal he and his friends had together (John 13).

When they arrived at the house, there was no servant on hand to greet them and to wash their feet for them — that would have been the normal, hospitable thing to do for any visitors. There was a bowl, a towel and some water available, but no-one seemed to be willing to do the necessary. But then, it was really the job of the most menial servant, so you couldn't expect any of them to do it, could you? It was beneath them. But it wasn't beneath Jesus: he didn't mind doing the servant's job. So he poured some water into the bowl, took the towel, and washed his friends' feet.

They were staggered, and embarrassed, and ashamed. Peter actually objected, but Jesus insisted. He was, he told them, setting them an example, an example of humility.

Contradiction or confirmation?

Unmistakable authority together with unsurpassed humility.

Some see this as contradiction, adding support to their denial of the divine claims of Jesus.

But there is another way to see it: that the great authority and the great humility of Jesus somehow combine in a beautiful and unique way to affirm the divine claims of Jesus.

For Thomas, one of the disciples, it took a while to see this. It was not till after Jesus had returned from death that it finally dawned on him. Confronted with the risen Jesus, and now convinced that he was alive, Thomas responded in the only way that made sense. 'My Lord and my God!' he said to Jesus (John 20:24–29). Jesus was to be acknowledged as Lord and worshipped as God.

And that is the way Christians have responded to Jesus ever since: because such is his authority that he must be Lord, and such is his power that he has to be God. Thus, from earliest times, Christians have confessed 'Jesus is Lord' and worshipped him as God.

Lord and God, or neither? What do you make of Jesus? How will you answer his question: 'Who do you say I am?'

7
Is there a future ?

What do you think about the future? Many, it seems, are very confused: there is a part of them which fears it; yet, at the same time, there is a part of them which is fascinated by it. Fear urges them to shut their minds to it; fascination drives them to find out all they can about it.

That is certainly true of today: the symptoms are all around us. Millions of people are avidly reading their horoscopes every day, many of them taking what they read very seriously. Increasing numbers are attracted by the prospects of having their palm read, or trying their hand with tarot cards; fortune-tellers seem to be in good supply too, particularly at our seaside resorts. (It is even possible to be given names and addresses over the counter in certain local advice centres.) Involvement in seances and other occult activities is common, and thought by many to be little more than a game, though, in reality, it is highly dangerous. Little do most of them realize that to dabble in such things is to risk being influenced by evil spiritual powers. Even children are involved, sometimes encouraged by teachers and youth leaders. On the political front, too, every so often a prophetic figure appears: he only has accurately to predict the assassination of a president, or a major disaster, or some other significant world event, and his services are in demand.

Ironically, it is often those most fascinated by the future

and driven to find out about it who end up most afraid of it. But why this interest? How much are we supposed to know?

The future: short-term
Jesus often spoke about the future, and he did so with considerable confidence and assurance. It was as if he had been given some insight into it, a glimpse at the master-plan. Usually, he himself featured prominently in the events he described, as if he were the all-important character around which everything would revolve.

Much of what he said surprised his friends, not least his description of the immediate future. He told them that he was going to suffer at the hands of religious leaders. That, in itself, should not have surprised them: he had so often run into conflict with them already, and they were gently fuming behind the scenes, critically watching his every move. But Jesus was in no doubt as to the outcome of this suffering: it would end in death. That both shocked and upset his friends, and Peter took him to task over it: 'Come off it — that'll never happen to you!' he said (or words to that effect — Matthew 16:22). Jesus put him very firmly in his place, actually accusing him of being the mouthpiece of the devil — not the sort of response you expect from a friend! Jesus obviously felt very strongly about the matter.

Later, Jesus told them more about his death. Although he would be accused and condemned by Jewish leaders, they would hand him over to others who would actually kill him. Previously, his enemies had tried to stone him to death; but Jesus was going to be crucified, the Roman form of execution reserved for the worst criminals.

And that is what happened: Jesus was arrested, tried (after a fashion), and condemned by the Jewish leaders; then taken before Pilate, the Roman Governor, who was persuaded to agree to his death — by crucifixion. But how did Jesus know all this in advance? Was it intuition? A feeling in his bones that this was how things would turn out? Or was he simply being particularly shrewd? With his past brushes with the law, the hostile atmosphere surrounding him, and the delicate political situation, you could say that there was a certain inevitability about Jesus' fate. Unless he changed his mind and took back some of the outrageous things he had been saying, it was difficult to see how a final clash with the authorities could be avoided. Anybody could see that. You don't have to be 'prophetic' or 'psychic', or anything else. So is there really any need for Christians to claim, as they do, that Jesus had some special God-given insight into the future?

In control

Clearly, Jesus made no attempt to avoid the inevitable: he actually spoke of suffering and death as something he 'must' go through, it was the whole purpose of his coming. 'That is why I came — so that I might go through this hour of suffering' (John 12:27). It was, as he saw it, all part of God's plan for him; nobody would have to twist his arm to make him do it — he would go willingly. Maybe he was taken by force and led off to be crucified, but it could happen only because he allowed it to. No-one really had the power to take his life from him: 'No one takes my life away from me. I give it up of my own free will. I have the right to give it up, and I have the right to take it back' (John 10:18).

What a strange way for anyone to talk about his death: that he is actually in control of when and how it happens. And if you read the accounts of his arrest, trial and death, it appears to be true. When Jesus is arrested he offers no resistance and the arresting soldiers hesitate to take him (John 18:1–14); at his trial before Pilate he has the audacity to tell the Roman Governor that he has authority over him only because it is given him by God (John 19:11); and when hanging on the cross, having provided for his mother's needs (John 19:25–27), he cries out to God: 'Father! In your hands I place my spirit!' Then, as if choosing his moment, he dies (Luke 23:46). It really leaves you wondering who was in control at his death: the Jewish leaders who plotted it, the Roman authorities who allowed it, the soldiers who performed it — or was Jesus in control the whole time?

Certainly, no-one has ever spoken about his own death in quite the way Jesus did. It was to be his great moment, the climax of his mission, the time when his glory would be revealed (John 13:31). What is more, his death would be the means of drawing many others to himself — 'When I am lifted up from the earth, I will draw everyone to me' (John 12:32). He actually believed that in dying he was laying down his life for others (John 10:15).

Strangest of all, perhaps, is Jesus' comment that the purpose of his coming was to give his life to redeem people, as a ransom (Mark 10:45). Now that was language the people of Jesus' day understood, because it was the language of the slave-market — slaves could be set free on the payment of a 'ransom price'. It ought to be familiar to us, too, living in these days of international terrorism, with prominent people being kidnapped and held captive while a ransom demand is made for their release. Jesus is making a peculiar claim: that his death is, in effect, the paying of a ransom which will secure the release of many people.

To Jesus, then, the immediate future was clear: arrest, trial and death. It was all planned, so that at no time would events be out of his control. And there was a marvellous purpose to it all: that many people (including us) might benefit.

Not the end

It is obvious that Jesus' friends didn't fully understand what he said about his death — at least, not at first. It is no wonder, therefore, that they were even more puzzled when he told them that his death would not be the end: that after three days he would come back to life again (Mark 9:31; 10:32-34). Even their great ancestors (e.g. Abraham, Moses and David), when they died, stayed dead; but here was Jesus boldly saying that he was different: he was going to return from death.

And that is just what he did. At least, that's what the records say he did, and that's what Christians have believed through the years. It may sound far-fetched, it is certainly original, but we believe it to be fact — a fact which many have tried to disprove, without much success. (We shall look at some of the evidence in chapter 9.)

Jesus knew it was going to happen and he tried to forewarn his friends. They didn't believe him, but he put the wind up his enemies: they made doubly sure the tomb where his body was buried was properly sealed and guarded (Matthew 27:62–66).

Jesus also made it clear that although he was coming back after his death, he wouldn't stay around for long. Eventually, he would go back to where he had come from. Just as Jesus had repeatedly talked of having come from God, of being sent by his Father, so he was equally insistent that he would return to God, that once he had completed what he came to do, he would go back to his Father. 'I am going to him who sent me . . . I did come from the Father, and I came into the world; and now I am leaving the world and going to the Father' (John 16:5, 28).

And so he did, and it's recorded in the book of Acts (Acts 1:1–11). We shall probably never be able to describe precisely what happened. For the disciples it was the last time they saw Jesus in the flesh on earth, and for Jesus it was the moment of his return to his Father. Christians remember it each year on Ascension Day.

Although Jesus was going, he would not leave his friends in the lurch: he didn't expect them to fend for themselves without him in the world. He promised that he would come to them again, though in a rather different way: his Spirit would come and live in them. That would be just like having Jesus there still. In fact, it would be even better: Jesus was close to them while he was with them 'in the flesh', but when his Spirit came he would be closer still, because he would actually be living in them. No doubt the disciples were puzzled: the prospects must have seemed both wonderful and fearful (John 14:16–18; 16:7).

Exactly what they expected to happen, if anything, we

don't know. But they waited for it, and it happened, ten days after Jesus had left them. The Spirit of Jesus came to that first group of Christians and filled each of them. And that's when it all started: the church, and Christians, and people talking about Jesus, and others being converted — it's been going on ever since.

The future: long-term

All that Jesus forecast concerning the short-term future happened. But he also looked further ahead, and spoke of the long-term future and of things which are still to happen. His track-record is so good it would be foolish to ignore what he says.

According to Jesus the one great event of the future, beside which everything else seems trivial, is his own personal return to this world. This time, his coming will not be in the insignificance of a Middle Eastern stable, but in great power and glory — the glory of God himself (Mark 8:38). What is more, his return will coincide with the end of the world as we know it.

Jesus warned his friends to be on their guard against those who came falsely claiming to be him — and there have been many of them over the years (Matthew 24:4–5)! There would be others who would claim to know the precise spot in the world to which Jesus will return, but they should be ignored — again, there have been those who have led people to beaches in Australia, and up mountains in Canada, and to a variety of other places to await Jesus' return (Matthew 24:26).

One thing Jesus made very clear: when he does come there will be no doubt about it and everyone will know. He also said that although there will be many signs which will indicate his imminent return, no-one will actually know the moment of his coming until he's there — Jehovah's Witnesses and others ought to take careful note of that whenever they try to predict the date of the end of the world. In fact, Jesus warned that his return would take place when people least expected it (Matthew 24:44).

What will his return mean? Judgment for all and permanent division between 'good' and 'evil' — Jesus told a number of stories to illustrate the point. He spoke of wheat and weeds growing together in a field until harvest, when the wheat is gathered into barns and the weeds are burned (Matthew 13:24–30). He told a story about some young girls waiting for the bridegroom to arrive for his wedding; some were ready for him and went in with him when he arrived, and some were not ready and found themselves locked out (Matthew 25:1–13). He compared judgment to a shepherd separating sheep from goats (Matthew 25:31–46).

But who will act as the judge? And on what basis will we be judged? I suppose most people who actually believe in some kind of judgment (and many don't, of course), assume that God will do the judging. Jesus' answer therefore comes as a surprise: God has given me the right and responsibility to act as judge of all (John 5:27). That means the eternal destiny of every one of us is in the hands of Jesus.

He's surely gone too far now. Is he sane, or has he got what psychiatrists would call 'a fixed delusion' about himself and the future? Imagine what would happen if I took to the streets and told everyone I met, 'Do you know, I am going to return to this world one day. When I do, I am going to judge you and that judgment will be final and irreversible!' If you had any sense you would have me locked away as quickly as possible to await psychiatric and social reports. Maybe that's what should have happened to Jesus for making such preposterous claims?

What about the future? Or would you prefer not to think about it? Horoscopes, crystal balls, tarot cards — those things may or may not be able to tell us something about the future, but if Jesus is right then he holds the key to the future for all of us. In fact, apart from him, there is no future worth talking about.

There are many today who are happy to acclaim Jesus as

57

one of the great world prophets. Yet how seriously do they take his 'prophetic' teaching concerning the future, the end of the world, his return, and his claim to be the judge of all? Christians take these claims of Jesus very seriously indeed; that's why they hail him as King of kings and look forward to his return as judge of all.

But are they right? What else can you say of a man who makes such claims as these? 'Who do you say I am?'

8
What a man!

I wonder how good you are at imagining what a person is like whom you have never met. Maybe you've heard about him, or read about him, and from what you have heard and read you try to build up a picture of the kind of person you think he is. How often does that picture have to be changed when you have an opportunity of meeting him? How often have you ended up saying, 'He's not at all like I imagined him to be'?

We have been considering some of the things Jesus said, some of the claims he made, trying to answer his question, 'Who do you say I am?' Whatever impression we may have gained of him, one thing is certain: we are not going to be able to check it out by actually meeting him and shaking hands with him. So, instead, we have to do the next best thing: examine his life closely. We need to understand the man as well as the message, to watch what he does and how he lives as well as listen to what he says, to try to get behind the words to his attitudes and motives.

The man and his message
If nothing else has emerged from our investigation of Jesus, I hope this much has: that any examination of the teaching of Jesus which is wrested from the context of the life of Jesus will be misleading; similarly, any consideration of the life of

Jesus which is divorced from the radical teaching of Jesus will be unbalanced.

The teaching alone could leave us with the impression of a somewhat forbidding, unapproachable, superior, religious person, because, as we have seen, so much of his teaching appears to be self-centred, intolerant, even arrogant.

Similarly, his life alone could lead us to the conclusion that in Jesus we have the human being *par excellence,* a great teacher, a wise counsellor, an excellent social worker, a champion of the disadvantaged and oppressed — indeed, that there is so much to admire and emulate in the man Jesus that any talk of divinity seems unnecessary and irrelevant.

But take the two together and neither of these verdicts on Jesus will be found adequate. The quality of his life will not let us dismiss him as a kind of self-centred religious fanatic (which some have tried to do), and the content of his teaching will not allow us simply to venerate a supreme human being (as many are content to do). Instead, as we have seen, we are forced to face up to a striking contrast — and it needs an explanation.

Contrasts

Whichever way you look at this contrast it is remarkable. There is Jesus' talk of an exclusive relationship with God which he alone has the right to invite others to share; yet, time and again, he demonstrates in his life an all-embracing love which seems to exclude no-one. He claims to be more than man, to be God's equal; and yet his life is the most completely human ever lived, full of compassion, sensitivity and down-to-earth love. At times, the things he says are horribly self-centred, calling people to himself, offering himself to meet people's needs, making demands of those who accept his offer; yet his life is a continuous demonstration of utterly selfless living, giving himself totally for other people whatever cost to himself. So outspoken was he at times that his teaching could be described as arrogant; except that in his life he displayed complete humility, even to the extent of doing a servant's job and washing his disciples' feet.

Has there ever been another man whose life has revealed such contrasts? Is there any parallel in history? There have been plenty who have made outrageous claims; but they haven't usually shown a great deal of humility. There have been those who were selfless in their living, giving themselves for others; but they have rarely, if ever, made claims which drew attention to themselves. In Jesus, it would seem, we have a unique combination.

Too good to be true?

There is one more thing, possibly the hardest of all for us to face up to, because it is foreign to us: we cannot imagine how any human being living on earth can be perfect. Yet, that is what Jesus claimed to be, it is what his friends said he was, and his life seems to confirm that it is true — he was without sin.

Clearly Jesus believed it. 'I always do what pleases him,' he said; and by that he meant that everything he did was according to God's will (John 8:29). So confident was he, that he even threw out this challenge: 'Which one of you can prove that I am guilty of sin?' (John 8:46). Apparently, no-one took it up. I wonder why?

Even at his trial they couldn't make any charge stick. They tried bribing witnesses, but their stories didn't tally (Mark 14:53–59). Pilate, the Roman Governor, had the same problem: he could find nothing against him. So he actually tried to have him released, not just once but five times. It was only when Jesus' enemies threatened to report Pilate to the Emperor that he gave way and allowed Jesus to be crucified (John 18:28 – 19:16). Publicly, he condemned Jesus to death; privately, he knew he was innocent. That's why he washed his hands in public, trying to show the people that he didn't really agree with what was happening (Matthew 27:24).

One of the criminals crucified with Jesus realized there was something different about him. For himself, he had been justly condemned; but Jesus — he had done nothing wrong (Luke 23:40-42). The army officer, responsible for the crucifixions that day, watched Jesus die. He had watched criminals die so many times before, but of Jesus he said: 'Certainly he was a good man!' (Luke 23:47).

We all know, to our embarrassment, that those closest to us, who know us best, usually know the truth about us. The close friends of Jesus, who had been with him throughout his public ministry, had the best opportunity of all to know him. John's verdict on Jesus was, 'There is no sin in him' (1 John 3:5); Peter's was similar: 'He committed no sin' (1 Peter 2:22). The earliest converts to Christianity were equally convinced about the sinless character of Jesus. Paul wrote, 'Christ was without sin' (2 Corinthians 5:21), and the writer of the letter to the Hebrews added that Jesus 'was tempted in every way that we are, but did not sin' (Hebrews 4:15).

All these people were close to the events of the life of Christ and their verdict is unanimous. Could they conceivably all be wrong? Or are they right? Certainly, Christians through the years have believed that Jesus was the only perfect man ever to walk this earth.

So what?
And what is the significance of that? It actually has a double significance.

First, it shows us up for what we really are. Many people have found Jesus difficult to cope with, disconcerting, unnerving. Somehow he is an embarrassment. Why? Because he is so good, too good — in fact, he's perfect. And that is hard for us to handle. His contemporaries certainly found that, so they had him crucified. I don't suppose we would have treated him any differently if we had been there. Jesus' perfect life will always challenge our imperfect lives. Of course, I can refuse to face up to him and then kid myself that I am a 'pretty good chap really'; but one look at Jesus and things look very different. The perfect life of Jesus shows us up for what we really are.

But, second, the perfect life of Jesus shows Jesus up for who he really is. One word used to describe God in the Bible (and it cannot really be used of anyone else) is 'holy'. That means utterly pure and clean, having no fault, no blemish, no sin. Religious people believed God was like that and they struggled to be like him. But Jesus *was* like God: he was perfect, without sin, holy. Could it be that his claim to be God really is valid and that it is confirmed by his sinless life? Christians would say 'Yes'. His perfect life shows Jesus up for who he really is: God.

Perfect man and holy God combined in one person, Jesus. That is the Christian claim. Paul was among the earliest Christians who saw this clearly. He wrote: 'Christ is the visible likeness of the invisible God . . . For it was by God's own decision that the Son has in himself the full nature of God . . . The full content of divine nature lives in Christ, in his humanity' (Colossians 1:15, 19; 2:9). The same truth was expressed in one of the early Christian creeds thus: 'We believe in one Lord, Jesus Christ, the only Son of God, eternally begotten of the Father, God from God, Light from Light, true God from true God, begotten, not made, of one Being with the Father.'

New Testament and creed alike are very explicit: Jesus is God. Christians, therefore, have good reason to believe it. Is there an adequate alternative answer to Jesus' question, 'Who do you say I am?'

9
'Who do you say I am?'

To consider the claims of Jesus too closely and for too long is a risky business, because there is a real danger that our preconceived ideas about him will be well and truly shaken, and our easy-going, complacent attitude to him threatened.

Certainly any ideas we may have about Jesus which are inspired by Christmas cribs, or by paintings of a blue-eyed, fresh-complexioned young man surrounded by a group of children, or by some of our well-known but 'soft-centred' hymns, begin to look rather threadbare and inadequate alongside the claims of Jesus we have been considering.

More than that, somehow Jesus seems to demand of us a decision about him one way or the other. No longer can we behave like the proverbial mugwump, who sat on the fence with his mug on one side and his wump on the other! Indeed, fence-sitting, which so many try to do, becomes a decidedly precarious occupation face-to-face with Jesus. He confronts us with his claims and demands of us: 'Who do you say I am?'

CHALLENGE NO 1: THE PERSON

We have looked at the different answers people have put forward to the question, 'Who is Jesus?' How reasonable do they seem now that we have considered Jesus' own claims?

Is Jesus simply one of the outstanding religious leaders of history, worthy to take his place alongside the other religious 'greats'? All of them, in their different ways, express truths: they all have something to say about our world, about man, and about our search for God. But if there is any truth in the teaching of Jesus about himself, then he must surely be in a class of his own.

Or is he a great man, perhaps the greatest ever to walk this earth? Certainly, there was a remarkable humanness about him, great compassion for human need, and great love for all people whoever and whatever they may be. But what man, however great, would dare to forgive the sins of others? What man could control the elements or raise the dead? And what of his claim to be God's equal: is that sheer delusion? If he was a deluded man how can he possibly be a great man? If his claims are true then he is much more than man; if they are not then he is much less than great.

Perhaps he should be acclaimed as one of the great prophets of human history, one who has brought something of God into the lives of men.

But there is a risk involved in declaring someone a prophet: it can be tested. And the test is very simple: is what he says true? If it's not, then he is no prophet. Ironically, according to some who hail him as a prophet, Jesus fails the test, because (so they claim) some of the things he says are not true. In particular, when he speaks of his relationship to God, he is not speaking truth from God — his claim to be God's equal is false. The trouble is, you can't have it both ways: either Jesus is a prophet speaking truth from God, or he is not. If what he says is untrue then he is no prophet; if all he says is true then he is more than a prophet.

Alternatively, he could be hailed as a great teacher. Clearly his teaching method was first class: he had that remarkable ability to teach profound things very simply. Above all, his ethical teaching has provided us with

65

unequalled moral principles which have proved themselves over the years.

Unfortunately, many who admire Jesus' 'moral' teaching seem to ignore his 'spiritual' teaching. They applaud Jesus when he says, 'Turn the other cheek', but ignore him when he says, 'No one goes to the Father except by me'; they happily repeat his command, 'Love one another', and conveniently forget his claim, 'I and the Father are one'. They make a personal selection from the teaching of Jesus, accepting what appeals and rejecting what does not appeal.

Is the moral teaching of Jesus more important than his spiritual teaching? Did he get his ethics right and his theology wrong? If his theology cannot be relied on, how trustworthy are his ethics? The two aspects of his teaching are so closely intertwined that it is unreasonable and arbitrary to separate them. Either he is right in both or wrong in both; in which case, he is either much more than a fine moral teacher, or he is not even that.

Through all these varying opinions about Jesus, his question still stands: 'Who do you say I am?'

In the end, Jesus' contemporaries had little doubt who he was. Peter, answering that question originally, said, 'You are the Messiah, the Son of the living God' (Matthew 16:16). Jesus commended him.

Martha of Bethany said, 'I do believe that you are the Messiah, the Son of God, who was to come into the world' (John 11:27).

Thomas, the doubting follower of Jesus, worshipped him: 'My Lord and my God!' (John 20:28). Apparently, Jesus accepted it.

Mark, when he began his account of the life of Jesus (probably the earliest account we have), began, 'This is the Good News about Jesus Christ, the Son of God' (Mark 1:1).

John, writing his account a little later, was even more direct: 'The Word (by which he meant Jesus) was the same as God . . . The Word became a human being' (John 1:1, 14).

The writer of the letter to the Hebrews said of Jesus, 'He reflects the brightness of God's glory and is the exact likeness of God's own being . . .' (Hebrews 1:3).

And Paul said of Jesus that 'he always had the nature of God' (Philippians 2:6) and that he 'is the exact likeness of God' (2 Corinthians 4:4).

There is a remarkable unity in the testimony of these early Christians. To them Jesus was more than a man, more than a fine teacher, more than a great prophet — he was God in human form.

Now you may be suspicious of this unity: you may think it could only be the result of an agreement between them; you may choose to discount their testimony because they were simple, gullible folk (provided, of course, you bear in mind that Paul was highly intelligent, being at least the equivalent of a university graduate); you may want to suggest any number of things to discredit this united testimony, but you need to have very good reasons for doing so.

And you still need to find an answer to Jesus' question: 'Who do you say I am?'

CHALLENGE NO 2: THE DIAGNOSIS

Although we must face up to the claims of Jesus to be God, we must not forget that he was man, and all the implications of that. He knew what it was to think and feel as a man, he could appreciate the pressures and problems that assail human beings, he even knew what it was like to be tempted like a human being. It was from this first-hand experience of life as a human being that Jesus considered man's plight and came up with a shrewd assessment of his real need.

Many today are ready with an opinion of the human predicament and some offer remedies too. Politicians point to the system and talk of reform; sociologists look at society and want to restructure it; economists call for new strategies, and ecologists for a fairer distribution of resources. There is a common factor in these conflicting opinions: man's problem is always someone else's fault.

Jesus sees things very differently: man's real problem is not something outside him, but something inside him — it's not 'them' or 'it' but 'me'.

He put it like this: 'It is what comes out of a person that makes him unclean. For from the inside, from a person's heart, come the evil ideas which lead him to do immoral things, to rob, kill, commit adultery, be greedy, and do all sorts of evil things; deceit, indecency, jealousy, slander, pride, and folly — all these evil things come from inside a person and make him unclean' (Mark 7:20–23).

Or, as one contemporary writer has helpfully summed it up: 'The heart of the human problem is the problem of the human heart.'

My experience of people, together with an honest appraisal of my own life, tells me that Jesus has got it right. Others have realized it too. Surprisingly, Bertrand Russell, a self-confessed atheist, is one. He wrote: 'It is in our hearts that evil lies, and it is from our hearts that it must be plucked out.'

The author G. K. Chesterton was another. He sent the shortest letter ever to the editor of *The Times;* it was in response to the question, 'What is wrong with the world?', and read,

> Sir,
>> I am.
>> Yours faithfully,
>> G. K. Chesterton.

If this is right then it's not new laws or new structures or new strategies that we need, but new hearts in people. We already have, for example, laws that can deal with a man who steals, or with someone who kills; but there is no law that can touch the greed that leads to theft or the hatred that ends with murder. It's changed hearts that are needed.

There is, of course, another name for the problem: *sin.* That is dismissed by many these days as outdated and irrelevant, but if you want to call a spade a spade, then 'sin' is the word. For sin is doing anything which goes against God's law. And what is that? Jesus summed it up for us when he said that the most important commandment was to love God with all you've got. (His actual words were: 'Love the Lord your God with all your heart, with all your soul, with all your mind, and with all your strength.')

There is a second important commandment: 'Love your neighbour as you love yourself' (Mark 12:29–31).

He is a bold man indeed who would claim never to have broken those commands — and if we've broken them, then, as far as God is concerned, we are guilty of sin.

But does sin matter? It does to God. And it matters, too, if you want to know God, because the one serious effect of sin is that it separates us from God. The same thing happens between friends: if I hurt a friend our friendship will be spoiled, and if it is not put right quickly there is a danger of our becoming separated.

Before God, who is holy, completely perfect, I stand condemned by my sin and in danger of being cut off from him because of it. Therefore, if I am to have any chance at all of knowing God, my sin must be dealt with first — and that I cannot do myself.

The interesting thing is that of all the many varying opinions in our world concerning the nature of man, Christianity alone is prepared to face up to the reality of man's sin — more often than not it is either ignored, excused, or explained away. But then Jesus is the only person who has ever claimed to be able to deal effectively and completely with man's sin.

Jesus' expert diagnosis of man and his need is as pertinent today as it ever was. And his remedy is still effective too!

CHALLENGE NO 3: THE CROSS

That remedy is the cross of Jesus. We have already seen the unusual way Jesus spoke of his death: that it was 'for others',

69

that as a result of it many would be drawn to him, that his death was in order 'to redeem many people'. But how is Jesus' death the remedy for man's sin?

John the Baptist, who came to prepare the way for Jesus, knew all along that Jesus had come to die for man's sin. That's why, when he first introduced Jesus publicly, he did so with these words: 'There is the Lamb of God, who takes away the sin of the world!' (John 1:29). That would remind his audience of animal sacrifice, a regular part of their religion.

What happened was that anyone wanting God's forgiveness for sin would have to bring an animal to the priest. It would be killed and forgiveness pronounced, forgiveness through and because of the animal's death. Of course, sin would come again and another animal would have to be sacrificed. But John was saying that Jesus was going to be sacrificed to deal with man's sin once and for all.

One of the early followers of Jesus obviously thought much about this and explained it thus: 'When Christ went through the tent . . . he did not take the blood of goats and bulls to offer as a sacrifice; rather, he took his own blood and obtained eternal salvation for us . . . he offered himself as a perfect sacrifice to God . . . Christ was offered in sacrifice once to take away the sins of many' (Hebrews 9:12, 14, 28).

Some of the other early followers of Jesus, although slow to understand at first, gradually appreciated the significance of Jesus' death. Peter put it like this: 'Christ himself carried our sins in his body to the cross' (1 Peter 2:24).

John wrote something similar: 'Christ himself is the means by which our sins are forgiven, and not our sins only, but also the sins of everyone' (1 John 2:2).

Paul explained it like this: 'Christ gave himself for our sins,' 'Christ died for the wicked' and 'it was while we were still sinners that Christ died for us!' (Galatians 1:4; Romans

5:6, 8). When Paul says that Christ died 'for' us, he means it was 'instead of' us, 'in our place'.

Here is the same united witness of the early followers of Jesus, this time agreed about the purpose and significance of the death of Jesus on the cross: it was for our sin. They are equally agreed about the effect of that death: 'Christ died . . . to lead you to God' (1 Peter 3:18); 'A better hope has been provided through which we come near to God' (Hebrews 7:19); 'We have been put right with God' and made 'God's friends' (Romans 5:1, 11). The effect of the cross of Jesus is to bring us into close relationship with God.

But why Jesus?

First, because, as we have already seen, if I am to know God something has to be done about my sin. There is nothing I can do about it; so God must do it. In Jesus, who is God, he has done it.

Secondly, because if anyone is going to deal with my sin, he ought to have none of his own to deal with. Only Jesus can claim that.

Why did he have to die? If God wants to forgive us, why can't he just let us off and forget it? He could, but then it would look as if sin didn't matter. But to God who is without sin, it matters very much, so much that it must always be punished — and the penalty is death. If that sounds harsh, remember that sin separates us from God and he is the source of all life.

Yet, God loves us; the last thing he wants is for us to be condemned to death. So, in the person of Jesus, he came to rescue us. He did that by taking our sin on himself and dying in our place. And that was a particularly crucial and effective move, because it serves a triple purpose: it shows God loves us; it takes sin seriously and sees that it is fully punished; and it offers us forgiveness, the problem of sin dealt with, and friendship with God possible.

But how is Jesus' death relevant today? Because it was

'once and for all' — for all sin, for all people, for all time. So you can enjoy its benefits now.

How?

First, by admitting that you are a sinner in need of rescue — that's what the Bible calls 'repentance'. It will be hard if you've always thought you were all right.

Secondly, by accepting that Jesus has effected that rescue for you, that you can't do it yourself but he's done it for you — the Bible calls that 'faith'. That will be hard, too, if you are the independent sort.

The cross of Jesus is the completely effective remedy for sin: and there is no other! As a result of it we may have our sin forgiven and removed, and be brought into a right relationship with God. Whether or not you believe that and accept it, one thing is certain: you cannot remove the cross of Jesus from history. It is indelibly written there and can never be erased. You can ignore it, dismiss it, laugh at it, consider it irrelevant, but you cannot remove it or undo it.

The cross stands today challenging us still to consider the one who died on it.

CHALLENGE NO 4: THE RESURRECTION

If the cross of Jesus is a challenge, the sequel is more so: that, although Jesus died on a cross, he didn't stay dead. A couple of days after his death and burial he reappeared, large as life, if not larger than life! It was recognizably Jesus all right, but he seemed to have acquired some remarkable and disconcerting powers — such as appearing and disappearing at will, even through locked doors.

Christians believe the resurrection actually happened. This is no myth or fairy story, no man-made happy ending to an otherwise sad story: this is straightforward historical fact. What is more, the resurrection of Jesus is the foundation for all that Christians believe and experience: without it our faith would be empty and our experience spurious.

Paul realized this. 'If Christ has not been raised from death, then we have nothing to preach and you have nothing to believe . . . If Christ has not been raised, then your faith is a delusion and you are still lost in your sins' (1 Corinthians 15:14, 17).

That's straight and to the point. Christianity stands or falls on the resurrection: take that one fact away and the rest disintegrates into a thousand pieces, and Christianity is finished. That means if you want to write off Christianity, then disprove the resurrection and the job's done! Not surprisingly, many have tried; unfortunately for them, none has succeeded.

This is not the place for a detailed account of the evidence for the resurrection: others have already done it well (see the booklist). Let us simply consider briefly some important aspects of it.

First, *the empty tomb.*

Even some who deny the resurrection admit that something happened to the body of Jesus so that the tomb was found empty on the first Easter morning.

One explanation, recently revived, suggests that Jesus never died but rather went into a deep coma; then, in the coolness of the tomb, he came to. But remember, Jesus had first been scourged, a punishment so vicious that some criminals died from it, then crucified, a process which often left every bone in the victim's body dislocated. Death was slow and painful, usually the result of asphyxiation.

In Jesus' case, death came quickly, and he was certified dead when a spear-wound in his side showed his blood beginning to separate. His body was taken down, wrapped up well, extravagantly embalmed, and laid in a tomb cut out of solid rock. The tomb was sealed with a large stone, and, because of Jesus' talk of resurrection, the authorities had it guarded.

After all that, you can, if you must, throw down the challenge: 'Get out of that!' But is it likely that Jesus survived death, revived and then escaped?

Some have suggested that the body was stolen, perhaps by the authorities. But why? It was in their interests to see that Jesus stayed dead: they wouldn't want to give his followers any excuse for claiming he was alive. And if they did take the body, what did they do with it? Why did they not produce it later when Jesus' followers started telling everyone he had risen? That would have put a stop to it!

Maybe the disciples took the body — that has been suggested. But it was easier said than done bearing in mind the precautions that had been taken over Jesus' tomb. Why should they want to take it anyway? And what did they do with it? What is more, if they had taken it, then we are supposed to believe that they were prepared to preach that Jesus had risen, to be arrested, beaten, imprisoned and killed for doing so, all the while knowing full well it was a lie. Is that really likely?

There is another thing that takes some explaining too: *the change in the disciples*. They didn't believe that Jesus would rise and were utterly disillusioned by his death — during the following days they were a sorry, frightened bunch of men. But in a very short while all that changed: they were on the streets fearlessly preaching about Jesus and saying he was alive. Something dramatic must have happened to cause the change. What was it?

And then there is *the church*. It began with that small group of Jesus' followers in Jerusalem and has spread throughout the world, surviving for 2,000 years, often through times of great difficulty, opposition and persecution. That needs an explanation.

Christians claim there is only one explanation that adequately fits the facts: that Jesus rose from death.

But why did he rise? What difference does it make? A great deal. To begin with, if Jesus had stayed dead, we might be able to dismiss him as some kind of religious crank or fraud. But if he rose from death, then we are forced to take him seriously. The resurrection is a sign that Jesus is who he claimed to be.

Secondly, if he had stayed dead, his death would be of little importance. But Jesus said, and Christians believe, that his death is of crucial importance: the means of dealing with our sin and making us God's friends. The resurrection is God's way of saying that Jesus' rescue bid has been successful, and that the benefits are now available to all. Paul put it like this: 'Because of our sins (Jesus) was handed over to die, and he was raised to life in order to put us right with God' (Romans 4:25). The death of Jesus is incomplete and ineffective without the resurrection.

Thirdly, if Jesus had stayed dead, it would have made nonsense of his claim to be the resurrection and the life, and of his offer of life beyond death. Does he really know what he's talking about? Can he prove it? The resurrection is Jesus' answer to those questions: 'Yes'!

One more thing: if Jesus has risen then he is still alive. And if he is still alive, then it is possible that his talk of returning as judge is not an idle threat. Certainly, the early Christians realized that: God 'has fixed a day in which he will judge the whole world with justice by means of a man he has chosen. He has given proof of this to everyone by raising that man from death!' (Acts 17:31).

The resurrection of Jesus is a dramatic demonstration that all Jesus said about himself is true. Of all things relating to him, some find this hardest of all to believe. Yet, it is the centre of the Christian's faith and the heart of the challenge of Jesus. It is therefore of crucial importance in answering Jesus' question: 'Who do you say I am?'

CHALLENGE NO 5: CHRISTIANS TODAY

The challenge of Jesus comes in one other way too: through Christians today who actually believe he is true. They believe he is God and accept his diagnosis of man's need; they have faced up to sin in their lives and realize they need to be rescued from it and its consequences; they acknowledge they cannot rescue themselves, so they accept that Jesus has done it for them, through his death and resurrection. As a result, they have committed their lives to Jesus, and have found that Jesus has, in a sense, committed his life to them — he has filled their lives with his Spirit, rather like he did for those first Christians 2,000 years ago.

This will seem strange talk to those who have not experienced it for themselves, but many who have will tell how they have met with the living Jesus. And that meeting has made a difference to their lives.

For some it has meant the removal of feelings of guilt, for others the end of fear of death; for some a new sense of belonging, for others a deep sense of peace. Some have discovered new love both for God and man, others have found freedom in areas of their lives where they had problems. All will speak of a new awareness of God, a new quality of life.

What is more, they are found in every continent, they come from every social background, they represent every level of intellectual ability; they are young and old, black and white, rich and poor; some are fit and healthy and others suffer incredibly. But they all claim to know Jesus personally.

Matthew is over seventy and stone deaf: he has met with Jesus, and it's obvious.

Jeff is a teenager and an electrical engineering apprentice; he has been changed through meeting Jesus — he knows it and so do his friends.

Kath is a young mother who has recently met with Jesus; the difference has been noticed by family and friends — and she doesn't mind telling them who has made the difference.

Martin was a drug user and only a few years ago sent to

Borstal for drug-pushing; he is now a Church of England clergyman.

University research scientists, bus drivers, housewives, steelworkers, teachers, unemployed — wherever you go you will find those who will tell you: 'Jesus is true, Jesus is alive.' They know because they are speaking from experience. And that is part of the challenge of Jesus.

But, in the end, you must decide for yourself.
'Who do you say I am?'

Book list

If you want to find out more about Jesus Christ and the Christian faith you could try any of the following:

Basic Christianity John Stott (IVP, 1971)
The Day Death Died Michael Green (IVP, 1982)
The Evidence for the Resurrection Sir Norman Anderson (IVP, 1950)
The Fact of Christ Sir Norman Anderson (IVP, 1979)
Is anyone there? David Watson (Hodder, 1979)
The Man from Outside Gordon Bridger (IVP, 1978)
This Jesus . . . David Day (IVP, 1980)
Who Moved the Stone? Frank Morison (Faber, 1944)
Why bother with Jesus? Michael Green (Hodder, 1979)